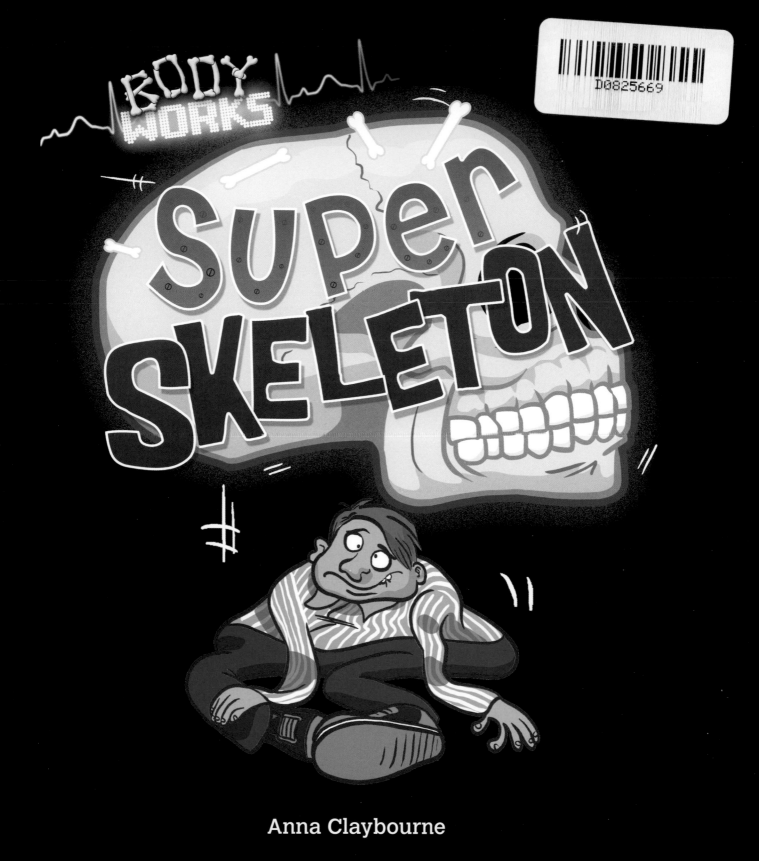

BODY WORKS

Super SKELETON

Anna Claybourne

QEB Publishing

Created for QEB Publishing by Tall Tree Ltd
Editor: Rob Colson
Designer: Jonathan Vipond
Illustrations, activities: Peter Bull
Illustrations, diagrams: Bill Greenhead

Copyright © QEB Publishing 2013

Project editor for QEB: Ruth Symons

First published in the United States by
QEB Publishing, Inc.
3 Wrigley, Suite A
Irvine, CA 92618

www.qed-publishing.co.uk

A CIP record for this book is available from the
Library of Congress.

ISBN 978 1 78171 598 7

Printed in China

Picture credits
(t=top, b=bottom, l=left, r=right, c=center)
Alamy 23b Fotomaton **Corbis** 14t Bettmann **Getty** 6l Dr Fred
Hossler, 27t Science&Society Picture Library, 30 Kean Collection
istockphoto 14-15 David Marchal **Shutterstock** 5t Palmer Kane
LLC, 5cl Teguh Tirtaputra, 5b watchara, 1, 6r itsmejust, 2, 7, back
cover Marcel Clemens, 8 Custom media, 9 Regien Paassen,
11 konstantynov, 12 cynoclub, 15t xpixel, 17 Robyn Mackenzie,
20-21 FXQuadro, 23t Artem Furman, 24-25 Zurijeta, 26 Marques,
27b Kutlayev Dmitry, 28-29 Dimj, 29b SergiyN, 29r Mari Swanepoel
SPL 5cr Patrick Landmann, 13t Gilbert S Grant, 13b Science Source

Note
In preparation of this book, all due care has
been exercised with regard to the activities
and advice depicted. The publishers regret
that they can accept no liability for any loss
or injury sustained.

Words in **bold** are explained
in the Glossary on page 31.

CONTENTS

WHAT IS A SKELETON?

Tap your forehead or squeeze your fingers, and you can feel something rock-hard just under your skin.

It's your skeleton—the solid framework of bone that your body is built around. Your skeleton does several very important jobs.

It surrounds delicate body parts such as your heart, lungs, and brain, keeping them safe.

It holds your body up and gives you your shape.

Some of your bones are **cell** factories, making blood cells for your body.

It bends and flexes, so that you can change position and move around.

SKELETON SMILE

Go to the mirror and give yourself a big smile. You will see part of your skeleton sticking out right before your eyes—your toothy grin! Turn to page 28 to find out more about teeth.

An octopus does not have a skeleton.

BONY BEASTS

If you look inside the body of a cat, a bird, a lizard, or even a whale, you'll find a skeleton that is similar to ours. Many smaller animals, such as insects, have a hard outer skin instead, called an **exoskeleton**. Some soft-bodied animals that live in the sea, such as octopuses and squid, have no skeleton at all.

A bat has five fingers, just like us.

An ant has an exoskeleton.

IMAGINE THIS...

What if you didn't have a skeleton? We are quite big, and we stand upright on long legs. Without our bones to hold us up, we'd collapse onto the floor like big blubbery bags of Jell-O.

5

YOUR SKELETON

An adult's skeleton is made up of 206 bones. Babies and children have even more—up to 300.

When you are born, your skull and pelvis are made up of many separate bones, which join or "fuse" together as you grow. In this picture, you can see the bones in a typical adult skeleton.

Why Do Bones Have Such Strange Names?

Most bones have Latin or Greek scientific names, based on what they look like. For example, the scientific name for the kneecap is "patella," which is Latin for "little pan."

Fibula

Metatarsals

Phalanges
or toe bones

Tarsals

Tibia

Patella
or kneecap

BIG BONES AND TEENY BONES

The bones of the skeleton range from big, heavy ones, such as those in the **skull** and the pelvis, to the tiny bones in your toes, fingers and ears. The biggest bone in the body is the femur, or thighbone, which can be 24 inches (60 cm) long in a tall adult. The smallest is the stirrup bone, found inside the ear—it's smaller than a pea!

Stirrup bone

ACTUAL SIZE!

There are
26 bones
in each foot.

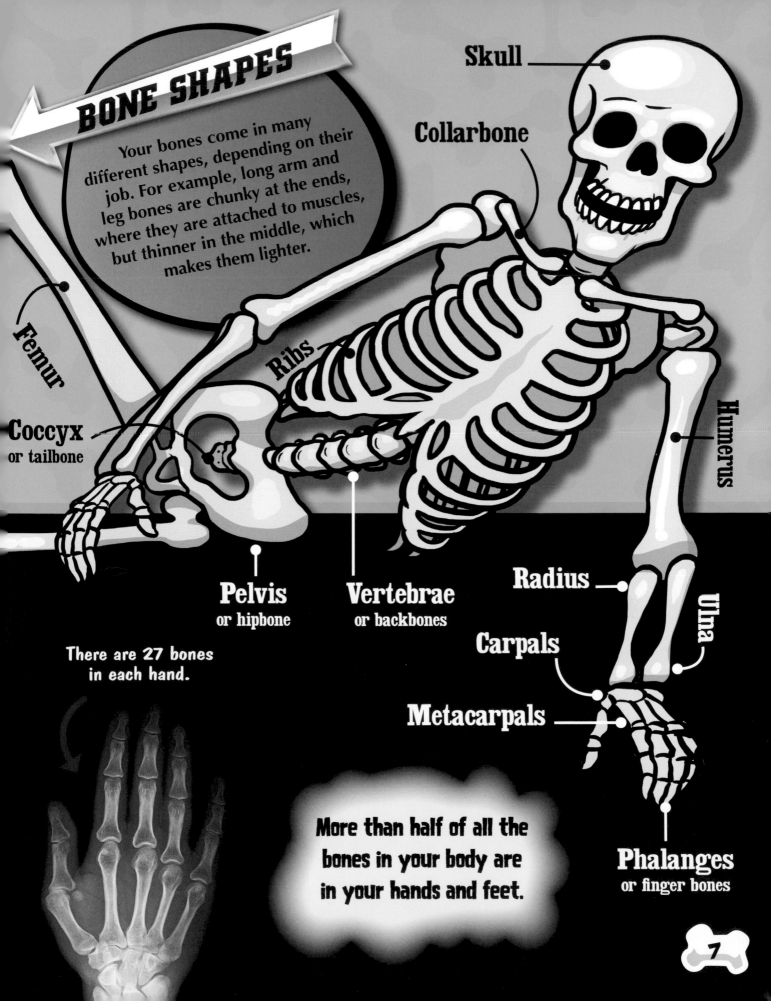

BONE SHAPES

Your bones come in many different shapes, depending on their job. For example, long arm and leg bones are chunky at the ends, where they are attached to muscles, but thinner in the middle, which makes them lighter.

Skull

Collarbone

Femur

Ribs

Coccyx or tailbone

Pelvis or hipbone

Vertebrae or backbones

Humerus

Radius

Ulna

Carpals

Metacarpals

Phalanges or finger bones

There are 27 bones in each hand.

More than half of all the bones in your body are in your hands and feet.

7

BENDY PARTS

Your bones are linked together by your joints. Some of the **joints** are fixed in place, but most of them can flex and bend.

There are different kinds of joint at different parts of your skeleton. Working together, they allow you to make all your everyday movements, such as running, sitting down, writing, and talking.

HINGE JOINT

A hinge joint works like a door hinge. It allows you to bend and straighten a body part. The elbow and knee are hinge joints.

RUBBERY PARTS

A tough, bendy material called **cartilage** is found in some parts of the skeleton, especially at the joints. Shown here in blue, it forms the cushions between the bones in your **spine**, and covers the ends of the bones so that they don't grind together. There's also a piece of cartilage at the tip of your nose, which is why it's slightly bendy.

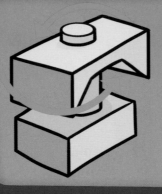

PIVOT JOINT

A bone with a sticking-out peg fits into a hole in another bone, allowing a circular movement. A pivot joint joins your skull to your neck.

BALL-AND-SOCKET JOINT

A bone with a ball-shaped end fits into a smooth socket. This allows it to move in many directions. Shoulders and hips are ball-and-socket joints.

Doctors can replace some types of joints if they are damaged or wear out. This is a replacement hip joint.

PAPER SKELETON

YOU WILL NEED:
- Thin white cardstock
- Tracing paper
- Pencil
- Scissors
- Hole punch
- 15 paper fasteners
- String

Make your own skeleton out of cardstock, and see how your bones all hang together.

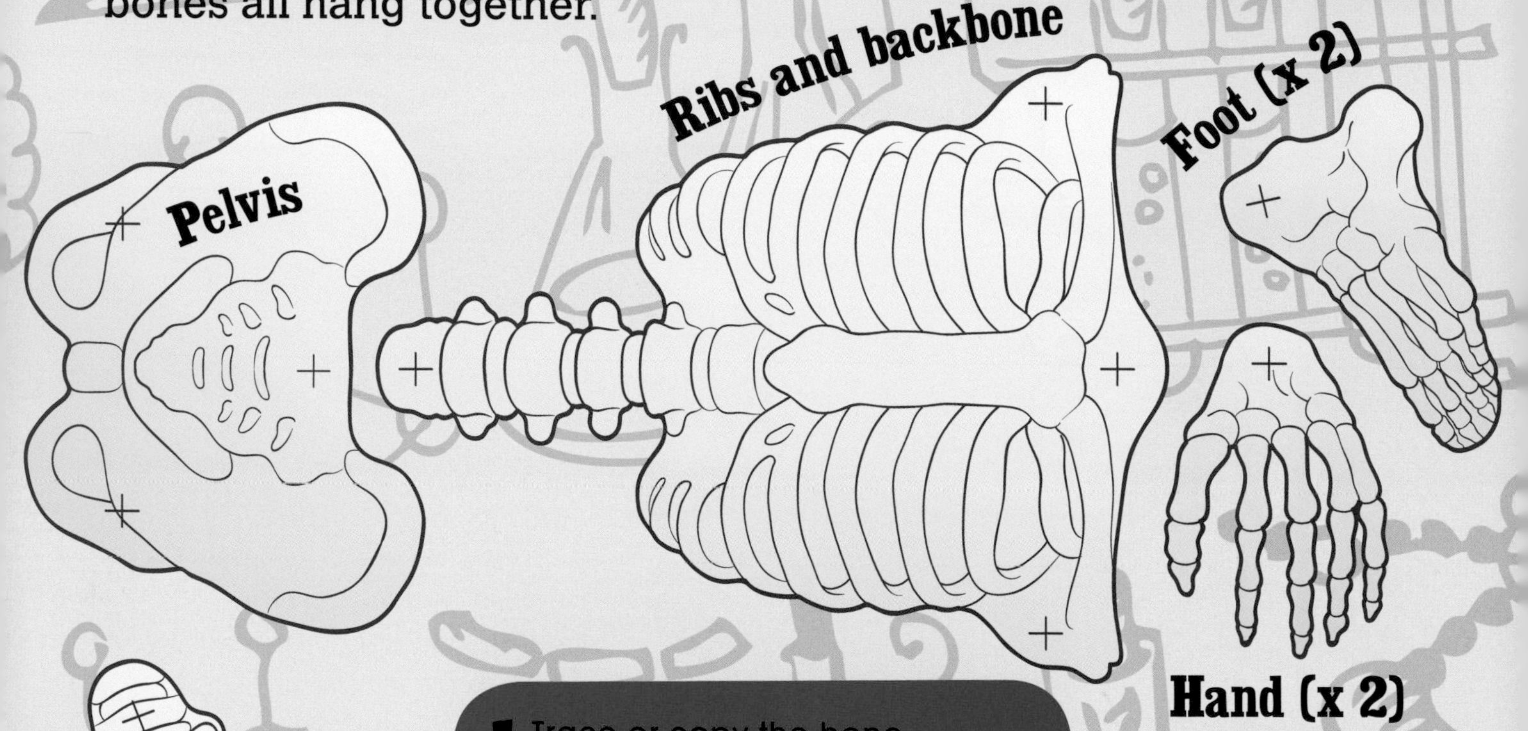

Pelvis

Ribs and backbone

Foot (x 2)

Hand (x 2)

Skull

1 Trace or copy the bone shapes shown here onto your cardstock, including the crosses at the ends of the bones. Draw on the extra detail showing the individual bone shapes.

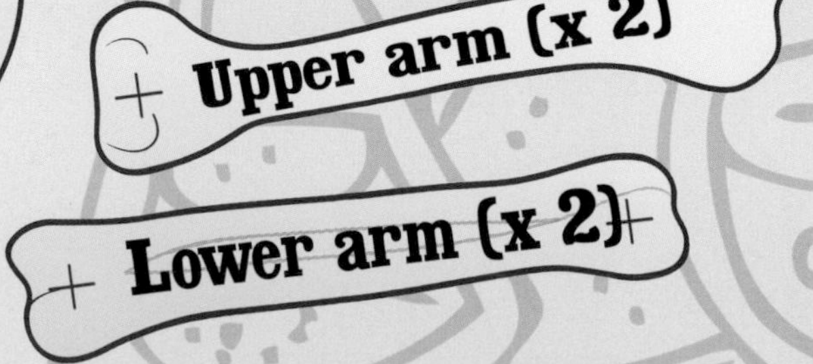

Upper arm (x 2)

Lower arm (x 2)

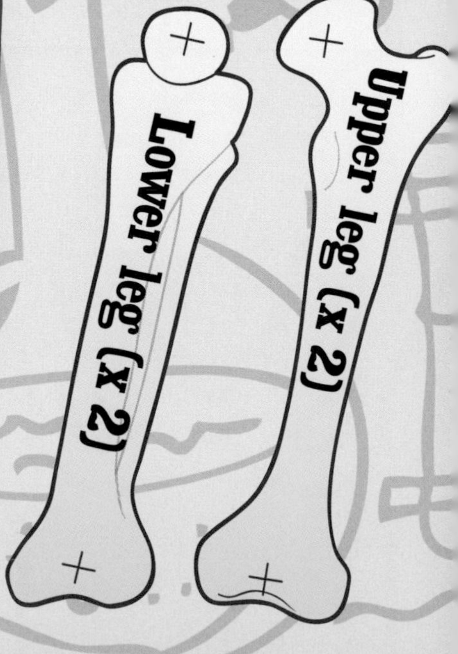

Lower leg (x 2)

Upper leg (x 2)

2 Carefully cut out the shapes. Use the hole punch to make holes where the crosses are.

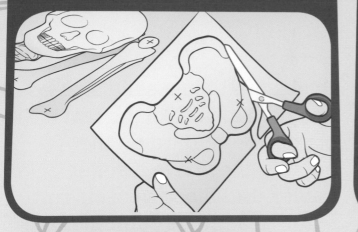

3 Link the pieces together at the joints using the paper fasteners. (If you forget what goes where, turn back to page 6!)

4 When the skeleton is finished, you can arrange it into any position you like. Thread a piece of string through the top so that you can hang it up.

Use glow-in-the-dark cardstock, or paint your bones with glow-in-the-dark paint, for a spooky nighttime skeleton!

Why Doesn't The Paper Skeleton Move Like Us?

Your paper skeleton can only move its joints sideways. This is how hinge joints like your elbows and knees work. We also need other types of joints that can move in different directions, such as a hip joint that can rotate.

INSIDE A BONE

STRONG AND SPONGY

Bones aren't just solid shapes. They are alive, like the rest of your body. Hard on the outside, they have a softer center, and **blood vessels** run straight through them.

Bones are made of several layers. They go from the hard layers of **compact bone** to lighter, bubble-like **spongy bone** on the inside.

Bone marrow

Periosteum

Nerve

Bone marrow is the soft, fatty substance at the center of large bones.

CELL FACTORY

Your larger bones contain a substance called **bone marrow**. It has a very important job—making new blood cells. The cells are released from the marrow into blood vessels (tubes that carry blood) and travel out into the rest of the body. Your bones make 3 million new blood cells every second!

TUBES IN AND OUT

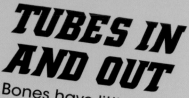

Bones have little holes and channels in them to hold blood vessels. Blood vessels carry food chemicals and **minerals** into your bones, so that they can grow and stay healthy. Bones also contain **nerves** (pathways carrying signals to and from the brain). Nerves tell your brain if your bones are damaged or broken.

BIRD BONES

Flying birds have hollow bones that are mostly empty inside. This makes their skeletons extralight, helping them get off the ground. Our heavier bones are one of the reasons why we humans can't fly, however hard we flap!

Compact bone

Blood vessels

Spongy bone

Spongy bone is full of bubblelike holes. But it's hard, not squishy like a real sponge. The spaces in spongy bone make your skeleton weigh less.

HOW DO BONES GROW?

By the time you are an adult, your bones will have grown to many times the size they were when you were born.

Your bones are growing in different ways, depending on how quickly they need to change size.

GROWTH PLATES

You get taller as a child because your **limb** bones grow very quickly. They have special **growth plates** near each end, made of rubbery cartilage. The plates make new cartilage and push it toward the middle parts of the bones. There, **calcium** and other minerals are added to it, and it turns into hard bone.

Joint cartilage

Growth plate

New cartilage forms on this side.

Cartilage becomes bone.

Robert Wadlow, the tallest man ever, grew to 8 feet 11 inches (2.72 meters). He was already 6 feet 6 inches (2 meters) tall by his 10th birthday!

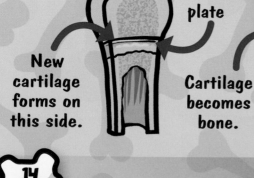

1 year   3 years   6 years

BROKEN BONES

If you break a bone, your body can repair itself. Over the course of a few weeks, a bone bridge forms across the gap. The bridge grows stronger until your bone is back to normal.

This arm has broken badly. It will take some months to heal.

Some bones grow more than others. Arm and leg bones get much longer, but the skull doesn't change size so much.

BONE BUILDING

Unlike your arm and leg bones, your other bones grow by a slower process called bone remodeling. Special cells in your body dissolve old bone. They build new bone in the gaps.

9 years   12 years   15 years

BENDY BONES

In this experiment, you can find out what your bones would be like without the calcium minerals that make them hard and strong.

1 Clean all the meat and gristle off the chicken leg and wash it well so that you are left with just the bone.

2 Fill the jar almost to the top with vinegar. Drop the bone in, and put the lid on.

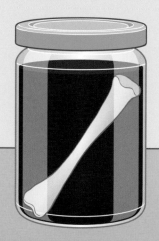

3 Leave the jar in a safe place for 5–7 days.

4 When the time is up, take the bone out and rinse it in water. Then try to bend it.

5 To double-check your results, check your main test against a second test. This time, take two bones. Put one in a jar of vinegar and one in a jar of water. Do they turn out differently?

What Happened?

Chicken bones are like our bones—they are hard and rigid because they contain a lot of calcium. Vinegar is a weak **acid**, and acids dissolve calcium. After a few days in the acid, most of the calcium dissolves. Without the calcium, the bone is mostly made up of soft substances and bends easily.

Broccoli

Milk

Salmon

Yogurt

Cheese

Nuts

Avocado

Skeleton Snacks

Food that contains calcium is good for you. Your body uses the calcium to keep your bones strong. The foods above are high in calcium. Which ones do you like?

Watercress

MUSCLE POWER

Your skeleton helps you move, but it can't do this on its own. It works with muscles, which are attached to your bones.

Our bodies contain three main kinds of muscle. About 640 skeletal muscles move and support the skeleton. Smooth muscle is wrapped around organs such as the intestines (to squeeze food along). The heart is made of cardiac muscle, which keeps it pumping.

PUUUUULL!

Frontalis

Deltoid

Pectoral muscle

Biceps

Abdominal muscles

Quadricep

Sartorius

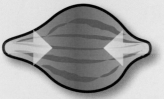

Relaxed muscle

Contracting muscle becomes shorter, pulling either side.

A muscle can only pull or relax. It cannot push. Muscles pull by **contracting**. When they relax, the muscles become longer again.

We use more than 300 muscles just to stand up!

THIS WAY AND THAT WAY

SInce muscles can only pull, most muscles work in pairs to make body parts move to and fro. For example, in your arm, the biceps muscle contracts to bend the elbow. The triceps muscle contracts to straighten it.

Triceps

Trapezius

Extensors

Hamstrings

Calf muscle

Gluteus maximus

Arm bends

Biceps contracts

Triceps relaxes

Arm straightens

Biceps relaxes

Triceps contracts

MUSCLE MAN

These pictures show what you'd look like if your skin were removed. You wouldn't see much of your skeleton at all, since the muscles cover so much of it. They are a dark reddish color and look like big bundles or cushions, fatter in the middle and narrower at the ends.

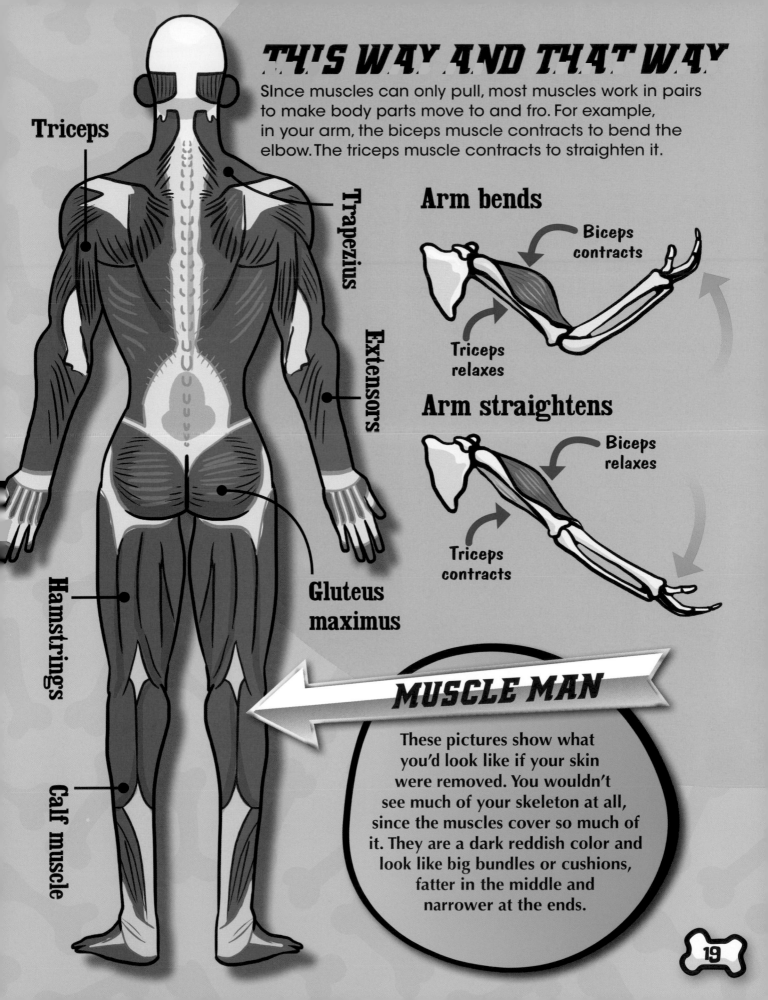

MUSCLE MODEL

YOU WILL NEED:

- Two 12-in (30-cm) wooden or plastic rulers
- Several small rubber bands
- Two elastic bands 4-6 in (10-15 cm) long
- Tape

This simple model of an arm works in the same way as your real arm muscles and bones.

1 in

1 in

1 Cross the two rulers over each other near the ends. There should be about 1 inch (2 cm) sticking out past the overlap.

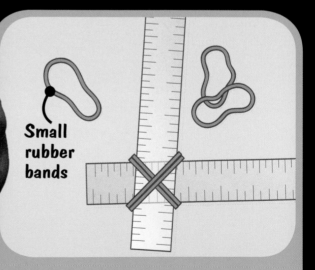

Small rubber bands

2 Loop a few small rubber bands around both rulers in a crisscross pattern. This will make an "elbow joint" that can move in both directions.

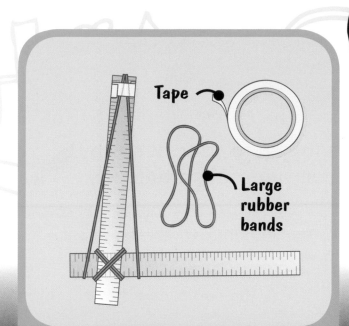

Tape

Large rubber bands

3 Take the two longer rubber bands and loop them over the lower ruler on both sides of the joint. Stretch them up and hook them onto the top of the upright ruler. Wrap a bit of tape around them near the top so that they don't jump off.

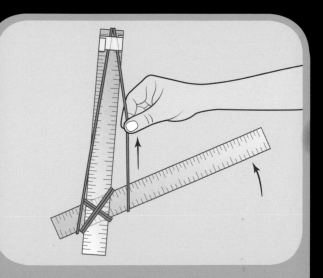

4 Now carefully pull on each of the rubber bands to make your model elbow joint flex up and down.

Why Do Bodybuilders Have Big Biceps?

If you use a muscle a lot, it starts to make itself stronger and bigger. So lifting weights and doing push-ups gives people bigger arm muscles.

What Happened?

The two long rubber bands work like the biceps and triceps muscles in your arm. When the biceps pulls, it makes the elbow bend. When the triceps pulls, it makes the elbow straighten.

STRINGY PARTS

Your muscles are joined to your bones by strong, elastic strings called tendons.

One bone is often attached to several different muscles. The tendons are very strong but thin, which means that there is room for several tendons to attach to the end of one bone.

Muscle

Tendon

Tendons attached to fingers run up to the arm.

FANCY FINGER WORK

Your fingers don't have muscles in them, since they would take up too much space. Instead, long tendons run from your fingers, through your hands, and up your arms. Muscles in your arms contract to pull on the tendons and control your fingers—just like strings pulling on puppets.

Finger bones

22

BOIIINNNG!

Calf muscles

Achilles tendon

Your calf muscles are attached to your heel bone by the Achilles tendon.

Heel bone

Try standing on one leg and hopping up and down. Your calf muscles are pulling your heel bone up, so you spring into the air. As you land, your Achilles tendon absorbs the weight of your body, so your heel doesn't crash into the ground.

Your Achilles tendon is the thickest, strongest tendon in your body.

This person has extremely stretchy tendons, allowing her to do this!

FLEXIBLE JOINTS

If you can bend your joints, such as your elbows and fingers, the "wrong" way, it's probably because you have extrastretchy tendons.

MAKE A
WORKING HAND

Pull the stringy tendons, and this model hand will curl up its fingers, just like a real hand.

YOU WILL NEED:

- Thin cardstock
- Scissors
- 5 non-bendable drinking straws
- Marker pen
- Tape
- String or knitting yarn

1 Draw around your hand onto the cardstock. Cut the hand shape out.

2 Take a straw and place it along one of the fingers of the hand. Make sure the end of the straw is at the fingertip. Mark the point where the base of the finger is on the straw.

3 Flatten the straw, and use the scissors to snip a triangle-shaped piece out of it on one side where the mark is. Make two more snips between the mark and the fingertip end of the straw.

4 Repeat steps 2 and 3 for the other three fingers, but make only two snips for the thumb. Then tape all the straws onto the fingers and the palm of the hand, with the snips facing upward.

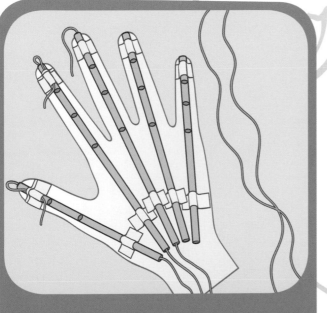

5 Cut 5 pieces of string about twice as long as the straws. Thread one through each straw, and tape the ends of the strings firmly to the fingertips.

6 Try it out! Hold the hand at the wrist and gently pull the five strings toward you.

BONES LEFT BEHIND

When a person dies, most of their body rots away, but the bones tend to stay around.

A skeleton can last for thousands of years, waiting to be discovered in an ancient cave or ruined castle. Dinosaur bones have been found that are many millions of years old!

Why Bones Last So Long

The bones in your body are alive, but they also contain a lot of calcium and other minerals. Minerals are nonliving substances found in rocks, and they don't rot. After death, the living parts of bone cells disappear, but the mineral parts are left behind.

WHY ARE BONES WHITE?

Calcium, one of the main minerals in bones, gives bones their whitish color. Calcium is also found in chalk, limestone, and seashells.

Just the hard mineral parts of the bones have survived in this ancient grave.

SKELETON STORIES

Some old skulls have holes cut through them. This was an ancient medical treatment called trepanation. People once thought it cured headaches!

Finding old bones can tell us all kinds of things about people from long ago. Experts can tell from a skeleton whether its owner was a man or a woman, their age when they died, and the diseases they suffered from.

IN PIECES

The joints that hold bones together rot away, so old skeletons are usually found as a pile of separate bones. When you see a whole skeleton in a museum, it's usually been pieced back together and fixed with wire.

This is the skeleton of a deer that lived thousands of years ago. The bones have been fixed back together.

ARE TEETH BONES?

Teeth are part of the skeleton, but they are not quite the same as bones.

They do a different job and have a different shape. However, they are made of similar substances, so skeletons get to keep their smiles!

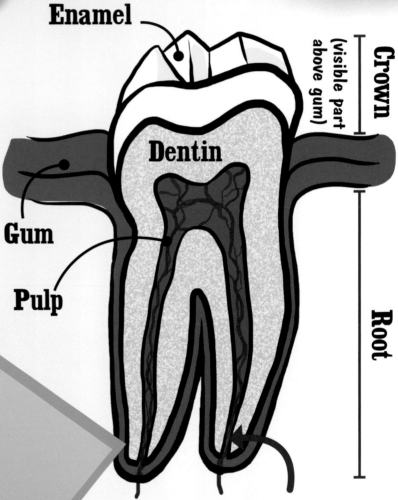

Enamel

Dentin

Gum

Pulp

Crown (visible part above gum)

Root

Nerves and blood vessels

INSIDE A TOOTH

An outer layer, called enamel, protects each tooth. It is the hardest substance in your body. Inside this is a strong bony layer called dentin. In the middle is the pulp, which contains blood vessels and nerves.

Your teeth sit in sockets in your jawbones.

TWO SETS OF TEETH

Your teeth first start to appear when you're around 6 months old—but these are just your first set, known as milk teeth. At age 6 or 7, they start falling out as the bigger adult teeth push through from underneath. We have two sets because teeth don't grow like bones. We start off with a small set and replace them with a larger set when our mouths have grown.

Why Do Teeth Need Brushing?

Teeth come into contact with food every day. **Bacteria** feed on leftover food. They make acid, which damages the enamel. Brushing your teeth gets rid of the leftover food and the bacteria.

MILK TUSK

Lots of other animals, such as cats and horses, have milk teeth. Baby elephants have milk tusks!

VIBRATING BONES

Inside your ear, sounds travel as vibrations along tiny bones. Most sounds enter the ear as soundwaves in the air. But some sounds enter through other bones in your body.

YOU WILL NEED:

- Two metal spoons
- String

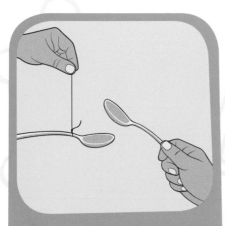

1 Tie the string to one metal spoon. Ask someone to hold the spoon up by the string and bang it with the other spoon. You'll hear a jangling sound.

2 Now hold the string between your teeth. Let the spoon hang down and get someone to hit it with the other spoon. Is the sound louder?

Can deaf people hear like this?

Some deaf people sense sounds using their bones. When the great composer Ludwig van Beethoven went deaf, he used a stick held between his teeth and his piano to hear.

What Happened?

When the first spoon was hit, the sound it made entered your ear through the air. When you held the spoon in your teeth, the sound entered your ear both through the air and through vibrations in your teeth and skull—so the sound seemed louder.

GLOSSARY

ACID
A type of chemical that dissolves some substances.

BACTERIA
Tiny living things that include some types of germs.

BLOOD VESSELS
Tubes that carry blood to every part of the body.

BONE MARROW
Soft, fatty substance found inside some bones, where blood cells are made.

CALCIUM
Type of mineral found in bones and teeth.

CARTILAGE
Rubbery, bendy material found in some joints and at the ends of some bones.

CELLS
Tiny building blocks that make up the human body and other living things.

COMPACT BONE
Hard substance found in a layer near the surface of most bones.

CONTRACT
To get smaller or shorter.

EXOSKELETON
Tough outer covering that some animals have instead of a bony skeleton.

GROWTH PLATE
Section of cartilage near the end of leg and arm bones, where new bone grows.

JOINT
Place at which two or more bones are connected to each other.

LIMBS
The arms and legs.

MINERALS
Natural, nonliving solid substances such as metals and precious stones.

NERVES
Pathways that carry signals between the brain and the rest of the body.

PERIOSTEUM
The outer layer of bones, where muscles, tendons, and ligaments attach.

SKULL
The bones that make up the head.

SPINE
The backbone, made of a series of bones called vertebrae.

SPONGY BONE
Light, honeycomb-like bone that makes up the inner part of some bones.

INDEX